My Life: Poem by Poem

D.M. Lippincott

To order additional copies of this book, contact:
Xlibris
844-714-8691
www.Xlibris.com
Orders@Xlibris.com

ISBN: Hardcover   978-1-6698-5357-2
       Softcover   978-1-6698-5176-9
       EBook   978-1-6698-5175-2

Print information available on the last page

Rev. date: 10/27/2022

Contents

Sleep

Have you ever tried going to sleep
But can't 'cause you're thinking about
The next day?

Or that thing that was said to make
Your husband go away?

Or why the kids didn't make it to
School that day?

Sleep ... why is it that I can't go?

Too much on my mind
Can't find the right position
I'm tired of lying on my back
I'm sick of being in this condition!

Why?

Why did you go?
It seemed too soon
All I could do was cry
If I would have known you were leaving
I would have said goodbye.

I knew you were sick
Just didn't know how bad
I wish I would have known
But now I'm feeling really sad

I had so much to tell you
So much to say
I never knew
It would have ended this way.

So much to do
No time to go back
They said it was all in your head
So little did they know
That you would wind up dead.

Life

To live is a gift
To die is a sin
But when you're handicapped
Where do you begin?

To see others worse than me
Makes me feel sad
I can't imagine how their condition
Makes them feel
I only know that it's very real.

And these illnesses
Whether it's MD, MS, spina bifida
Or anything else that can
Rot the human body
Should be a sin
But no one's at fault
Where do we begin?

Decide and *choose*
Are two hard words
To decide to live with what you've been given
Or to choose not to
Is the real sin

To Live

Should I stay
Or do I go?
What difference would it make
And who would know?

Living shouldn't be this hard
I often do it with a smile
I try so hard to stay positive
I can only be that way for a while

I used to do everything
A superwoman of such
And now I can't do anything
And it tears me up so much.

Life

Did I tell you about the life I'm in?
Let me say it really sucks
Oh, where do I begin?

Married at nineteen
Thinking it would last for years
And then I became a little jealous
I wanted to be out with my peers.

At twenty-two I met a great guy
He made good money
Thinking my life was gonna be wonderful
And that he was gonna be my honey.

In 1992 I bought my first house
Got married again and had my first son
Life was gonna be good
We'd only just begun

Why Me?

When I do it, I knew it's my fault
When they do it, it's still my fault
Why is it I should be the one to blame
And end up carrying all the shame?

If something should ever happen to me
Please do not cry
Just smile and be happy
For now I am free to fly.

I'm sure my husband just
wishes I were gone, dead
He gets so mad at me
He doesn't respect me and
treats me like a schoolchild
And I only wish it were my
problems he could see.

He's as sensitive as a rock
And chauvinistic to boot
I'm sure that when it comes to me
He doesn't give a hoot.

He says I do nothing,
that I'm totally lazy
Which is so not true
Tell me, if you lived a
3,200 sq. foot home
Where would you start,
what would you do?

I am just so tired, so worn out
Like sometimes I can't go on
I'm sure he'd be so much happier
With me totally gone.

And sometimes I feel like
I'd be better off
Being totally gone
And that he'd be able to
get a lot more done
And then the war of the Lippincotts
Would finally be over
And he would have won.

He hasn't said "I love you"
I can't remember how long
But then again how would you feel
If someone was telling you that
you were always wrong?

He is warm as a snow pea
His words cut like ice
I just don't understand
Why he isn't very nice.

I just don't know
I really can't tell
I don't think I'm going to heaven
I've done died and gone to hell.

Why?

I hurt him once
With my words
I never meant to say
I'm hoping he'll still hold me close
And not hold me at bay.

Why did I say it?
What was I thinking?
Why do I always hurt the ones I love?
Can't think, can only cry
Afraid he's going to say goodbye.

I want to be with you
I love you so much
I love your arms around me
I yearn for your touch.

I'd like us to always be together
Please don't leave me
I'm sorry, I'm sorry
Please forgive me, can't you see?

I trust you, I trust me
And together we shall always be
Happy today, happy tomorrow
Happier still and forevermore.

Normal

What is normal?
How is normal to be
I thought I acted normal
I was only being me.

I don't know what the future holds
The future seems unclear
I do know one thing
That to me you are very dear.

I have MS
MS does not have me
And I've got it by its thorns
The day we met
Was the day my love for you was born.

I don't have answers
I only have books
And I read all I can
Please let me read with you
To make you a stronger man.

Someone

You've been through a lot
I see that now
And don't want to scare you away
I have just grown to love you
And continue to do so every day.

I don't need a supporter
I don't need a crutch
I just want to be with you
I love you so very much.

An ear to listen
A shoulder to cry on
Strong arms to hold me tight
To keep me safe and warm at night.

Someone to walk with
Someone to laugh with
Someone I'd vow to never hurt
You are that someone
And with you my life has just begun.

I don't know where we're going
Or if and when it will end
One thing, though, is for certain
I would always want to remain your friend.

Live

Have I ever asked you
What it means to live?
Is it about all you can get
Or how much you can give?

Do you listen
And truly understand?
Or do you walk away
Without lending a hand?

Have you ever had it all
A big house, a big boat, a big car
And then wonder why?
What's all this stuff for, who am I to impress
When all you want to do is cry?

Living simply, not needing much
I don't need a lot
I just need enough.

I may be handicapped
Trapped in my own body
And trust me, I don't want to be
I just want to be like everyone else
I want to be me!

All I can say
Is live life to the fullest
And whether you laugh or cry
Tomorrow is another day!

Refuse

I refuse to give up
In this game called MS
I'd hate to lose; I want to win
This game called MS
It really should be a sin.

I refuse to give up
I'm gonna keep walking and talking
And do what I do
I'm gonna say "To hell with MS
And shame on you!"

I refuse to give up
You, MS, may have taken away
My ability to drive, swim, and dance
But MS, you'll never catch my spirit
'Cause I'll never give you the chance

I refuse to give up
And, MS, you may be with me forever
You won't stop me or slow me down
'Cause you're not that clever

I refuse to give up
'Cause where there's a will, there's a way, I say
And I do get things done
And you, MS will not win
'Cause I've already won!

Life

Some have long ones
Some have short ones
No one really knows why
And all I know is it makes me cry.

Life can be good
Life can be bad
Sometimes, really, though
It can be sad

Life with MS
Can sometimes be a challenge
And that really sucks
All I'd really like to do
Is to go out and earn a few bucks!

Failure

You wanna marry the man of your dreams
He gives you the ring he bought
You make plans, reservations, commitments
It would be wonderful
At least that's what you thought.

You join a church from birth
And grow to learn, love, and believe
Oh, all the things there is to know
Why is it you just don't go?

You join a business venture
Hoping it'll make you money
They say "Just bring us people
And we'll sign 'em up for ya, honey."

Nothing ever works right
Whether it's the car, my body, the store
And trying to fix whatever it is
Can be such a chore.

Nothing ever gets done; I'm just not that fast
Hurry up, hurry up, I need it now
Or maybe you can show me how
'Cause right now I'm not gonna last.

MS

If MS had a hand
It might help me stand
Instead it waits there
Waiting for me to fall from my chair.

If MS were a person, someone you could touch
I'd ask him, "Why did you have to infect so many good people?"
I'd wait for his response, and if I didn't get one
I'd say, "I've never hated something so much!"

It has taken my ability to walk, dance, run, swim, hike, climb
But I know in my heart that this, too, will pass
It's just a matter of time.

I often think I'd like to make it go away
But it's made me who I am today
Besides, having MS isn't all that fun
Now all I do is write poems and pray.

Having MS is so not very fun
I'll often think of life
Sit down to cry
And think, *I'm done!*

MS Really Sucks

MS really sucks
It can make you mean and gruff
I won't let it win
It'll only make me tough.

MS really sucks
It takes away your freedoms
Things you want to do, and need to do
And nothing can get done.

My legs won't move, my knees get stuck
I can't even climb into Millie's truck.

MS really sucks!
I can't even get out of bed
I fling around like a fish out of water
Wishing I were dead.

MS really sucks
I wish there was a cure
Maybe by the time I'm gone
It won't be here anymore.

MS really sucks
It takes things away
I often think about what I can't do
And it makes me cry every day

Balls

Take life by the balls
And don't be afraid by who knows
And if they have anything to say
Just tell 'em, "That's the way it goes."

Take life by the balls
You've just got to
One day you're gonna succeed
That's just you've got to do.

Take life by the balls
You often don't care
What the world thinks
'Cause life is often too much to bare.

Take life by the balls
As only you can
You were better before this illness
And now you know where you stand.

Take life by the balls
And give 'em a good pull, squeeze, and shake
You're gonna make a difference in the world
As only you can make.

Take life by the balls
As this, too, will pass
And if anyone makes fun of you
Tell 'em all to kiss your ass!

MS = More Shit

I used to walk with my head held high
But MS took my ability to walk straight
Using a walker to walk
I often feel I've got a prostate.

I've always wanted to make others laugh
Not cry
But in the end I know they'd wonder
Why did she have to die?

MS stands for multiple sclerosis
MS to me stands for more shit
More this, more that
Unable to do more of this crap.

Forty-Five

I'm only forty-five
I want to live my life
But when my MS gets in the way
It gives me nothing but strife

I'm only forty-five, I don't want to die
It's hard to think, sometimes even blink
That tomorrow I could be in the sky.

It's just impossible getting dressed
Or getting my shoes and socks on
If you were waiting for me
You'd for surely be long gone.

Like taking a shower, now that's a real trial
Try taking it with someone, you'll be sure to
be in there awhile.
But dropping the soap, it's so hard to chase
slip and slide, back and forth
Then you wonder, what is this really worth?

Living is so hard
Dying is a cinch
I often think it's where I need to be
In there, lying in a ditch.

I know it's a reality
Not yours, but mine
And know that it sucks to be me
And that it'll all end
In a matter of time.

Dinner

What's it mean really?
To have a meal late at night
To eat alone
To eat a meal with the family
Just to give the dog a bone?

To make a meal
Is more than a few ingredients
You need to mix, stir, and stand
For you're about to make something grand.

To make anything
You must first be able to stand
So you can mix and stir, slice and dice
Otherwise you'll make something
Not so nice

Before you can stand
You must have balance
You have to stand to walk, cook
Or dance.

MS has taken away a lot of things
My ability to stand, to walk, to dance and cook
But I'm gonna do my best to continue cooking dinner
'Cause MS you should know by now that I'm the winner!

June 25, 2019

MR and MS

Mister and misses are quite a pair
From where they came
And with no name
For this is no game.

M is for mental
R is for retardation
It's something in the brain
That isn't quite right
It might make you walk funny
Talk funny, be funny
And you know when
you're just bung you
Knowing you have nothing
to gain or lose.

M is for multiple
S is for sclerosis
Hardening of many tissues
Including arms, legs,
hands, feet, and toes
It's real hard to try re-
bending any of those.

You're as stiff as a corpse
late at night while
Trying to sleep
Unable to move, change
positions, to scratch that itch
But do you dare make a peep?

Now MR is fun
'Cause it's fun when you're dumb
While MS is always stiff
Having a hard time getting
anything done.

Now MR and MS had a great life
They never had any stress nor any strife
When you've got one that's
always in agreement
And the other acts as though
they're in cement
How can you not make
a funny comment?

Fat

Fat—what's that?
It's that extra bulge
You were never looking forward to
But when you sit around like a rock
You can't help but indulge

To be fat is just not me
I don't like the way I am
It's not so much what I eat
It's that I just can't move
I really just want to get back in my groove.

I exercise and do what I can
To keep the fat in check
I just refuse to stay in the shape I'm in
So I just say, "What the heck!"

Chores

Having to do a chore
Can really be a bore
And knowing that it has to get done
Why not make it fun.

Take out the trash
Make the bed
Mop the floor
And if you're feeling a little crazy
and you want to get up and dance
Who said chores are no fun
And take that chance.

Not Now

I don't want to die
I don't want to go
Please say it's just not right
Please say it isn't so.

I'm happy here
I want to stay
I have a lot of living to do
Like to see the sunset in the bay.

My kids are raised
They're all grown
They hold a special place in my heart
It's too soon to go
I want to stay and not depart.

Cry

Why cry?
For loss
For pain
For sorrow
For happiness
For misery
For keeping bad company?
The list can go on and on
But it certainly won't keep
You make up on.

To have a love one tell you
They don't love you and
That it's time to move on.

To have a loved one die
Unexpectedly or one that was ill
And was expected and has
Passed on.

The beautiful wedding
The beautiful baby
The unexpected news of cancer
And no one has an answer.

We pray for a reason
We fight to stay alive
We have a will to be
We all must have that drive.

And if things only get worse
For no unknown reason, we cry
We cry for the answers
We cry for the pain
And when we see no end in sight
We cry again.

Rock

A pebble, a rock, a stone
To step on one will hurt you to the bone.

To be unable to do anything
To sit all day and stare
Is like a rock
And a little more than I can bare.

To be a decorated ornamental rock
In someone's yard
Or to be on a mountaintop
And then being pushed off
Wishing you could yell "Stop."

Sit sit sit—that's all I can do
It's boring as all hell
And really I'd rather be visiting
With friends like you.

Stuck

Stuck—what's that mean?

Are you stuck in traffic
In a bad relationship
Or in a dead end job?
Or worse yet, are you feeling like a slob?

Wherever you've stuck
There's always a way out
Now try being stuck in your own skin
With no way out!

Try being stuck in the bathroom
You can't get off the seat
'Cause there's nothing to grab to pull you up
And then realizing you're the only one home
There is no help.

How about being stuck in a chair
You wanna go here, you wanna go there
Unable to move 'cause you're not strong enough
Can make your day seem bleak
And just when you think it can't get any worse
You accidentally take a leak!

Happy

What's it mean to be happy?
To wake up with a smile
And get on your on with your day
And be on your merry way.

To wake up and greet the sun
To say "Good morning, oh beautiful one."

Is it a state of mind or a choice?
Some might say it's both
To choose to be in a happy state of mind
Is choosing to be one of a kind.

Be delightful, cheerful, and hopeful
For life is so unpredictable
You might not know where to begin
So when you do, start with a grin!

Smile

You hear someone call your name
You turn around to say hello
And you smile.

The phone rings
It's an old friend
You answer it
With a smile.

Smiles happen when familiar voices are hear
Smiles happen throughout the year.
Smile do not happen
When you hear the crash of a tear.

Bathroom

Every one's got one
You kinda have to
It's for going number 1
Or number 2.

You use a bathroom for many reasons
To shave, read, or bathe
No matter how long you're in there
You're always ready to leave

Now let's say you're home alone
And you're in that room
You've done your business, you're done
You try to get up, can't, and it's not fun.

Now let's say
You're stuck to that darn toilet seat
So you move back and forth in a wiggly
sort of way
And then you realize the toilet seat broke
And you've landed on the floor
In the most peculiar way.

Me

Hi, my name is Deena
I have MS
I used to be an organized person
Now I'm just a mess.

I'm generally a happy person
I enjoy making people smile
Or to get a little laugh
Even for a little while

I used to have a spring in my step
Well, now I no longer have a step
But I've still got a spring
Even if it's a string kinda thing

I've been married; I've got three boys
They're quickly turning into men
Doing great things, I hope
'Cause Lord knows I can't begin again.

21, 2020

In a Day

Day in and day out
What's it really all about?
To have all day to just sit in a chair
Can be too much for me to bear.

To sit all day I guess I could knit
Knit a sock or two
For me, nah
That just won't do.

Never a day in my life
Did I ever expect it to be like this
'Cause all I really want is to stand up
And give you a real hug and a kiss.

MS

How dare you come into my life
And take my abilities away
Things I did every night
And every day.

Right now I'm not doing well
You've put my life
Straight in hell.

My legs are stiff
My hands are enclosed
Never in a million years
did I think I'd be like this
Who would have thought?
Thank you, MS.

What did I do to you?
Where did you come from?
You should have opened my hand
And inserted a gun.

That's just how I feel
I know it's not real
But you, MS, must go
'Cause I'm the one that's gonna win this show.

MS

How dare you enter my life
And take my abilities away
Things I did every night
And every day
I'm now unable to do.

Right now I'm not doing well
You've put my life straight through hell.

My legs are stiff
My hands are in fists
I never thought MS would
be like this
And now I'm feeling like rigor mortis
is setting in
So I'm thinking, you, MS, are about to win!

Printed in the United States
by Baker & Taylor Publisher Services